Usborne
Wipe-Clean
Horse and Pony Activities
Illustrated by Manola Caprini
Designed by Laura Hammonds
Written by Kirsteen Robson
Consultant: Rosie Dickins
Use your wipe-clean pen to do all the activities in this fun-filled book.
6 7 8 9 10
I0820449

In the field

Connect the numbered dots in order, to finish the farmhouse.

Draw 4 more spots on the pony above.

Draw over the dotted lines to finish the ponies.

Use the pen to fill in the tractor wheels.
Spot 3 differences between Bramble and Hazel.
Hazel
Bramble
Find and circle 5 rabbits.

Riding school

Write an X under the pony that does not match the others.
Rory
Count the poles on each jump below, then trace over the numbers.
1
2
3

In the stable yard

Draw tails on the horses below that need them.

Find and circle 6 birds.

Draw over the dotted lines to finish this pony's saddle.

Connect the numbered dots in order, to finish the stable.

Follow the trails to see who will brush their way to the wheelbarrow.

Countryside trail

Use the pen to show these riders the way back to the stables.

Count the rabbits in each group, then trace over the numbers.

Draw over the dotted lines to finish the trees.
Write an X by the duck that does not match the others.

In the stable

Draw a line between each pair of matching kittens.

Spot 3 differences between the two wheelbarrows below.

Find and circle 2 mice.

Draw over
the dotted lines
to finish the
horses.
Rufus
Nyobi
Lottie
Follow the trails
to see what each
person will pick up.

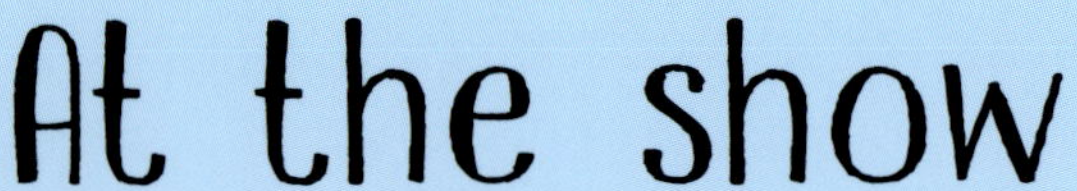

At the show

Write an X under the van below that does not match the others.

Sally

Use the pen to show Sally the way to the showjumping competition.

Find and circle 10 white flowers.

Connect the numbered dots in order, to finish the horse trailer.
3
4
5
2
1
7
6

Showjumping

Spot 5 differences between Phillip and Stefan and their ponies.

Draw over the dotted lines to finish the jumps.

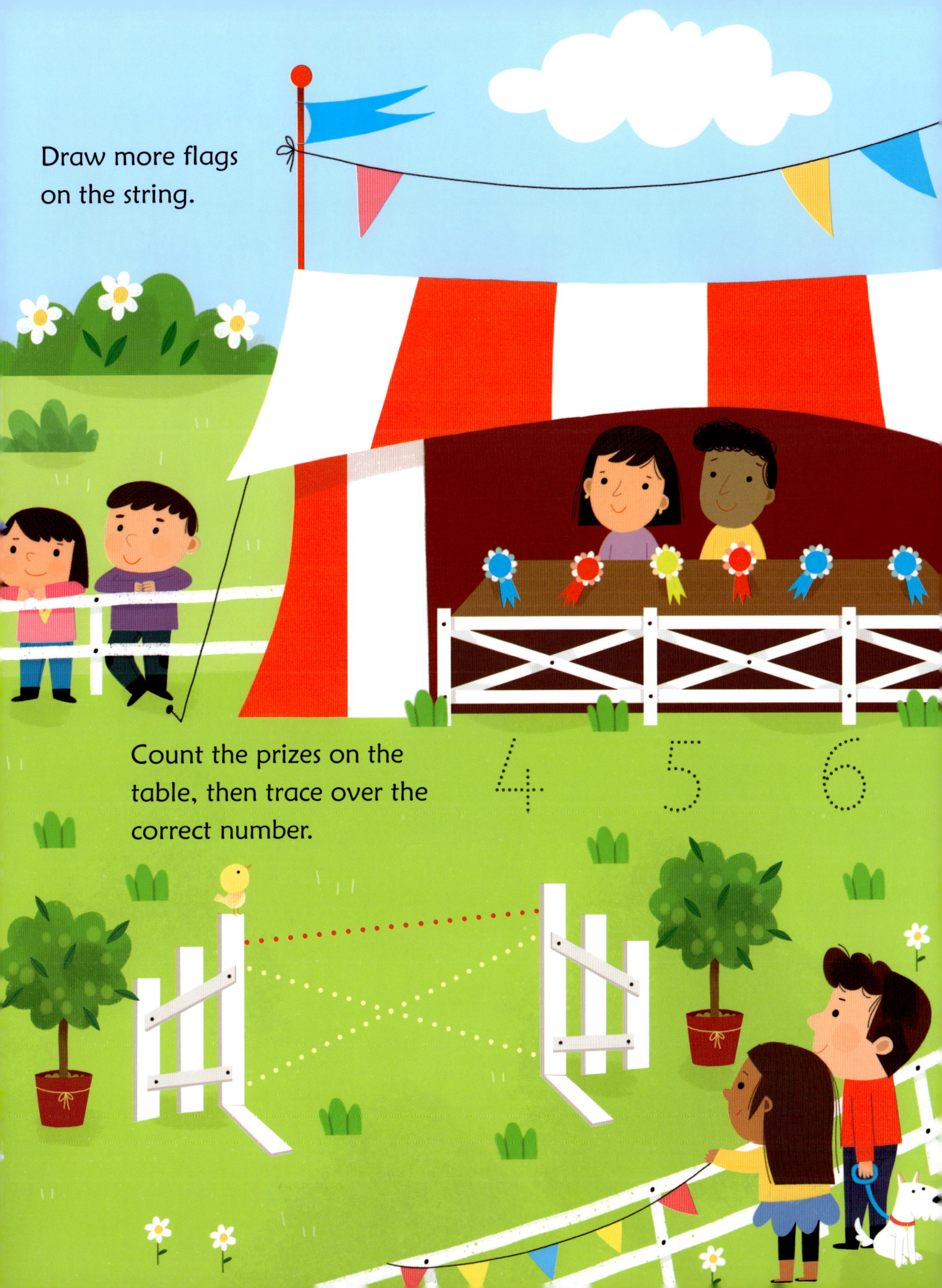
Draw more flags on the string.
Count the prizes on the table, then trace over the correct number.
4
5
6

Fun and games

Draw over the dotted lines to finish the flags.
Find and circle 2
blue riding hats.

In the tack room

Write an X above the jacket that does not match the others.

Draw over the dotted lines to finish the three stirrups on the saddles.

Count the boots below, then trace over the correct number.

Spot 5 differences between the things on the shelves.
1ST
1ST
Connect the numbered dots in order, to finish the winner's cup.
4
5
3
6
2
7
1
8

Camping out

Draw a line between each pair of matching tents.

Follow the trails to see who will sit on each log by the fire.